PET GUIDE

Care for Your Hamster

D0565744

Contents

HarperCollins*Publishers*
1 London Bridge Street
London SE1 9GF

www.harpercollins.co.uk

10 9 8 7 6 5 4 3 2

First published 1985 as *Care for your Hamster* by William Collins Sons & Co Ltd

This new edition published 2015

Front cover image: RSPCA
Photographs: RSPCA except for AlexKalashnikov/shutterstock.com p15; Allocricetulus/shutterstock.com p9 (right); Andrew Forsyth/RSPCA p28 (top); Andy Lidstone/shutterstock.com p28 (bottom); Becky Murray/RSPCA p16, 44 (top); Cynoclub/shutterstock.com p9 (left); Damion Diplock/RSPCA p42 (top right); Elya Vatel/shutterstock.com p5; Emilia Stasiak/shutterstock.com p9 (centre); FomaA/shutterstock.com p43; Haveseen/shutterstock.com p31; Hintau Aliaksei/shutterstock.com p25; Joe Murphy/RSPCA p39; KPG_Payless/shutterstock.com p27; Kristina Stasiuliene/shutterstock.com p30; LeonP/shutterstock.com p19; Lepas/shutterstock.com p11; LIUSHENGFILM/shutterstock.com p23; Marina Jay/shutterstock.com bottom p34; P/shutterstock.com bottom p42; Photogal/shutterstock bottom p44; Pitroviz/shutterstock.com p41; Ruslan Kudrin/shutterstock.com p35; Stock_shot/shutterstock.com p7, 17, 22,24, 29, 40, 42 (top left); Su Jianfei/shutterstock.com p34 (top); Tikhonova Yana/shutterstock.com p21; Top: Damion Diplock/RSPCA p18; VeryOlive/shutterstock.com (bottom) p24 (bottom); Vishnevskiy Vasily/shutterstock.com p8 (right)

This book has been compiled on the basis of expert advice and scientific research. To the best of our knowledge it is correct at the time of going to press. The information contained in this book is intended only as a guide. If you are unsure, or you have any concerns about your pet(s), you must speak to a vet, who will be able to give you advice that is appropriate for your individual animal(s).

The Animal Welfare Act 2006 applies to England and Wales. Similar separate legislation covers Scotland and Northern Ireland, so owners must fulfil the same legal duties of care.

A catalogue record for this book is available from the British Library

PB ISBN 978-0-00-811830-3

Colour reproduction by Born

Printed and bound by RR Donnelley APS

MIX
Paper from
responsible sources
FSC
www.fsc.org
FSC C007454

FSC™ is a non-profit international organisation established to promote the responsible management of the world's forests. Products carrying the FSC label are independently certified to assure consumers that they come from forests that are managed to meet the social, economic and ecological needs of present and future generations, and other controlled sources.

Find out more about HarperCollins and the environment at
www.harpercollins.co.uk/green

Foreword

O wning a hamster can be incredibly rewarding and a great source of companionship. Pets can provide opportunities for social interactions, helping people feel less lonely and isolated. Growing up with pets also offers health benefits, and caring for an animal can help improve a child's social skills, encouraging the development of compassion, understanding and a respect for living things. Having a hamster is, however, a huge responsibility and requires long-term commitment in terms of care and finances.

Before getting a hamster, it is important that time is taken to discuss the commitment and care required with all family members, and that everyone agrees to having and looking after a hamster in the home. Bear in mind that once you have your hamster there is a legal requirement under the Animal Welfare Act 2006 to care for them properly, so you must be sure that you will be able to do this throughout your hamster's life. This means providing somewhere suitable for them to live, a healthy diet, opportunities to behave normally, the provision of appropriate company, and ensuring that they are well.

If you are able to care for a hamster properly and make the decision to go ahead, then please consider giving a home to one of the many hamsters currently in the RSPCA's animal centres throughout England and Wales.

This book is based on up-to-date knowledge of hamster behaviour and welfare approved by the RSPCA. It has been written to provide you with all the care information you need to keep your hamster happy and healthy throughout your lives together. We hope you enjoy it.

Samantha Gaines BSc (Hons) MSc PhD
Alice Potter BSc (Hons) MSc
Lisa Richards BSc (Hons)
Jane Tyson BSc (Hons) MSc PhD
Animal behaviour and welfare experts, Companion
Animals Department, RSPCA

Introduction

Owning and caring for a hamster can be great fun and very rewarding. But it is also a long-term commitment and a big responsibility in terms of care and cost. Typically hamsters live for around two years, but some may live longer. You will need to think carefully about lots of different things to decide whether you are able to give a hamster the care and attention they need. Here are some of the things you need to consider:

Hamsters are nocturnal

This means that they spend most of the day sleeping and become active in the evening and late at night. Because of this, they can make good pets for people who may be out during the day and at home in the evening. It also means that they may be less suitable for young children, as they will miss the hamster's most active periods.

Hamsters have quite complex needs

Despite their small size, hamsters have quite complex needs. You must think very carefully about whether keeping a hamster fits in with your family and home life. You need to make sure that you can meet all their welfare needs, which includes feeding them every day, spending time gently handling them and keeping their home clean, as well as making sure your hamster doesn't get bored.

Hamsters are very active animals

At night, when they are most active, they can be quite noisy. They will spend time climbing, digging, burrowing and gnawing. Make sure you have enough space in your home for a suitably sized cage that you can place in a quiet location. This will give your hamster the peace and quiet they need, as well as ensuring that your pet's night-time activities don't disturb you or your family.

Hamsters need responsible care

Although hamsters are often seen as being ideal pets for children because they are small and have plenty of character, it is vital that an adult is responsible for ensuring that the pet's needs are met. Adults will also need to supervise children when they are holding a hamster, because these little animals can be easily injured through careless or rough handling. Children will need careful instruction and help to learn how to handle their pet gently and safely.

Hamsters are a long-term commitment

Typically, hamsters live for around two years, although some may live longer. Think very carefully about whether you can afford the cost of feeding and caring for a hamster over that period of time. Some of the things you will need to consider are the cost of a suitable home for them, food and bedding, equipment, vet bills and insurance. You must also make sure that a responsible person can look after your pet whenever you are away.

The Animal Welfare Act

Under the Animal Welfare Act 2006, it is a legal obligation to care for animals properly by meeting five welfare needs. These are: a suitable place to live; a healthy diet including clean, fresh water; the ability to behave normally; appropriate company; and protection from pain, suffering, injury and illness. This care guide contains lots of information and tips to help you make sure these needs are met.

LIFE HISTORY

SCIENTIFIC NAME Syrian (or golden) hamster: *Mesocricetus auratus*

CAMPBELL'S RUSSIAN HAMSTER *Phodopus campbelli*

WINTER WHITE RUSSIAN HAMSTER (DJUNGARIAN OR SIBERIAN) *Phodopus sungorus*

ROBOROVSKI HAMSTER *Phodopus roborovskii*

CHINESE HAMSTER *Cricetulus griseus*

GESTATION PERIOD 15–22 days (approx.)

LITTER SIZE Varies, average of 3–10 (approx.)

NAME OF YOUNG Pups

EYES OPEN 14–15 days (approx.)

WEANING AGE 21–30 days

PUBERTY 42–100 days (approx. depending on species). Can be as early as 3–4 weeks in Syrians.

ADULT WEIGHT Varies with species from 20–180g (1–6.3oz) (approx.)

LIFE EXPECTANCY Up to 2 years, but some may live longer (approx.). Males tend to outlive females.

Note: These figures are guidelines only and will vary for individual animals.

Choosing the right type of hamster for you

If you are certain that you will be able to care for a hamster, the next stage is to do plenty of research to decide which type of hamster is right for you.

Type

Although in the wild there are more than 24 types of hamster, only five are kept as pets. You can find out more information about these five types of hamster on pages 8–9.

Age

If you have decided that a baby hamster, or pup, is suitable for your family and lifestyle, you will need to make sure that, as well as being happy and healthy, they have been weaned and are ready to leave their mother. The right age for this varies depending on the species and individual animal, but it is normally at around 3–4 weeks old.

Sex

Personal taste apart, there is very little significance in the choice between male and female hamsters. Female Syrian hamsters tend to be slightly larger than males. Some species, such as Syrian and Chinese hamsters, are solitary and should be housed alone, whereas other types, such as Winter White Russian hamsters, naturally live in groups. If you are going to house hamsters together, this should be done only with advice from your vet or from a specialist rescue organization, whose staff should be able to help you even if you have not adopted hamsters from them. If you are housing hamsters in groups, a single-sex group is best, to avoid unwanted pregnancies.

Size

Hamsters vary in size. The Roborovski hamster can be just 4–5 centimetres long while larger varieties, such as Syrian hamsters, can be around 18 centimetres long. Because of their small size, hamsters need to be handled extremely gently and with great care.

Health

Whatever type of hamster you are thinking of getting, it's important to find out what health, behaviour and physical issues they may be vulnerable to developing. As well as causing pain and suffering to your hamster, a propensity to certain conditions may also mean expensive bills for veterinary treatment. Knowing which types of hamster tend to have fewer problems will give you the best chance of getting a happy, healthy pet.

Take time to
select the right
hamster.

Types of hamster

Hamsters originated in Asia and the Middle East and have been popular as pets for many years. They have stocky bodies, thick, soft fur and large cheek pouches. Like many pets, they come in a range of colours and coat types and there are several different types that are popular. Some people may like a particular type of hamster because of their looks, but do try to look beyond these generalizations, as every hamster has its own unique character and temperament. The way hamsters behave will depend upon how they are reared, cared for and treated. All hamsters need appropriate care, company and a suitable diet and environment to be happy and healthy.

There are five types of hamster that are most commonly kept as pets: the Syrian and four types of dwarf hamster.

Syrian (or Golden)

The Syrian hamster originated in the Middle East and is a popular pet, but sadly it is now endangered in the wild. They are solitary animals, so they should always be kept alone, as even littermates are likely to fight as adults. Although Syrians tend to be golden brown, there are lots of variations in the colour of their coats, from white to grey or chocolate brown. Long-haired Syrian hamsters need grooming every day to stop the fur becoming matted. Satin types have smooth, glossy coats, while Rex Syrians have wavy coats and curly whiskers.

Campbell's Russian

Campbell's Russian hamsters are mostly brown, albino (white with red eyes) or sandy-coloured. Like the other dwarf species, Campbell's Russian hamsters come from Central Asia. As well as short-haired types, there are also Satin types, with smooth coats, and the Rex, which, like Rex Syrians, have wavy coats and curly whiskers.

Campbell's Russian hamsters can be prone to diabetes, so always ask about this before you buy one.

Winter White Russian (Djungarian or Siberian)

Winter White Russian hamsters are sometimes known as Siberian hamsters and are a close relative of the Campbell's Russian. Winter White Russians come in a variety of colours, the most common being black and grey, blue-grey or white. They get their name because their fur turns white in winter – in the wild this helps them to stay hidden in the snow. Although Winter White Russians can live in groups, they should be monitored carefully if quarrels occur, so that fighting and injury are avoided.

Roborovski

Roborovskis are the smallest type of hamster and are usually brown and white. Unlike Syrians, they are sociable animals and should be kept in pairs or groups with the advice of your vet or rescue organization. Roborovskis tend to be very active and they can squeeze into the tiniest of spaces. They can be very fast movers, too, which means handling them can be difficult.

Chinese

Chinese hamsters are the largest of the dwarf hamsters; they tend to have longer tails and most have brown fur with a distinct black stripe running down their back. They can be very territorial, so, like the Syrian hamster, it is advisable to keep them in separate cages. Chinese hamsters can be affected by diabetes, so this is something to consider before buying one.

LEFT TO RIGHT: Syrian; Campbell's Russian; Winter White Russian; Roborovski; Chinese.

Getting a hamster

Where to buy

You may have decided what size, sex and type of hamster is most suitable for your family, but you should then take your time in selecting the right individual pet.

The RSPCA encourages anyone looking for a pet to consider taking on one of the thousands of animals it rescues each year. Rehoming charities often have hamsters of all different types and colours looking for a good home, some of which will be bonded groups.

If you are planning to buy your hamster directly from the person who bred them, do some research first to make sure that you choose a responsible breeder. Breeders should be happy to discuss with you subjects such as how the hamsters have been kept. Wherever possible, you should try to see the baby hamsters (pups) with their mothers, as this will give you a good picture of how well they have been cared for, and seeing the parent will also give you a fair indication of the hamster's eventual size and sociability.

If you are going to buy a hamster from a pet shop, be sure to buy from an outlet that meets all the welfare needs of the animals in their care and also ensures that this information is freely available for potential owners.

Meeting your hamster

Before you go to see a breeder, it is a good idea to call first. A good breeder will be happy to talk to you and answer any questions you may have. When you visit, look for signs that the litter (and parents) seem healthy and well cared for. If you feel that anything is not quite right about the situation, it may be best to walk away and choose your hamster from somewhere else.

Information

A reputable breeder should supply you with information to help you to care for your new hamster. This should include telling you about how they have been looked after by them. It is particularly important to find out about your hamster's diet and in particular what types of food they are used to. Ideally a breeder should provide you with a week's food for your hamster, too, as any sudden changes to your hamster's diet could make them ill.

Finding a healthy hamster

Wherever you view your hamster, you should always check that they are healthy. Here are some signs that may indicate that a hamster has an underlying medical problem:

- Not eating or drinking
- Sitting in a hunched-up position (this could mean they are in pain or unwell)
- Sunken or dull-looking eyes
- Drinking lots of water
- Wet faeces and/or diarrhoea (which may lead to soiling of their bottom)
- Discharge from the nostrils, eyes or vagina
- Persistent sneezing or coughing
- Persistent scratching, especially if focused on one area
- Firm, warm and swollen stomach
- Abnormal lumps and bumps on the body
- Weakness, wobbliness or difficulty standing up
- Difficulty walking or not using a limb
- A dirty coat that is tangled or matted

These are just a few examples. If you notice anything at all that doesn't look quite right with the hamsters you have seen, you may want to consider getting your pet from somewhere else. If you have concerns about the welfare of any of the animals you have visited, call the RSPCA (details can be found at www.rspca.org.uk).

ABOVE LEFT: Check the hamster is healthy.
LEFT: Pet shops house littermates together. Once older they may need to be housed individually.

Biology

Rodents

Hamsters belong to the rodent family, which includes other animals such as rats, mice, gerbils and guinea pigs that are also kept as pets. In the wild, rodents include the squirrel, dormouse and capybara. The feature that all rodents have in common is their teeth, which are especially adapted for gnawing. In fact, the word rodent comes from the Latin word 'rodere', which means 'to gnaw'.

Exaggerated features

Some types of hamster have been bred to emphasize certain physical features, which over time have become more exaggerated. Although these may be seen as 'normal' for a specific breed, some features may cause problems. For example, long-haired hamsters can have problems grooming and may be more prone to a condition called 'wet tail'. They may also get their long hair trapped in their wheel, which can be painful and distressing. Try to ensure that any hamster you choose is free from exaggerated features.

Cheek pouches

Hamsters have folds of skin in their mouths called 'cheek pouches'. These are important for survival in the wild, as they help hamsters to store food they find while foraging over a large area until they can take it back to their underground homes to digest it. When the cheek pouches are full, it makes the sides of the face bulge out – sometimes the bulge may stretch as far back as the shoulders. Cheek pouches are separate from the mouth and have quite a delicate lining. It is important not to put anything in your hamster's home that may damage the pouches, such as straw.

Teeth

Like other rodents, such as guinea pigs and rats, a hamster has long front teeth called 'incisors', which grow continuously. It is important that you make sure your hamster can wear their teeth down to keep them healthy. Hamsters love to gnaw and need lots of things to chew. Putting a gnawing block in your hamster's home will help them keep their teeth at the right length (for more on gnawing blocks, see page 31). Even so, it is important to check your hamster's teeth at least once a week, and if you notice any problems, seek veterinary advice immediately.

Eyes

Healthy hamsters have bright, alert eyes with no signs of crustiness or discharge around them. Hamsters have excellent hearing and a very keen sense of smell, but their eyesight is quite poor, so they rely more on their other senses to find food. Because of their poor eyesight, you should always be very careful not to startle your hamster, as they may bite if frightened.

Coat and whiskers

A healthy hamster will have a clean, glossy coat with no bald patches, sores or lumps under the skin. Hamsters use their sense of touch and their whiskers – which help to detect objects and low-frequency movement – to explore their environment. A hamster's whiskers vibrate backwards and forwards up to 30 times per second in short bursts; these movements are known as 'whisking'. This action sends important information to the hamster about objects that are close to them that they may not be able to see, due to their poor eyesight.

Scent glands

Hamsters have dark spots on each hip; these are scent glands, which they use to mark their territory. This scent-marking is particularly important because, having poor eyesight, hamsters rely greatly on their sense of smell.

Feet and claws

When hamsters are feeding they tend to stand on their back legs, holding the food in their front paws. They also use their front paws to put food into their mouths. Usually hamsters' claws wear down naturally, but they should be checked regularly to make sure they are not damaged or overgrown. If they are, speak to your vet.

Environment

1

All hamsters need a nesting box.

A suitable place to live

Before you bring your hamster home, make sure you have prepared a suitable, safe place for them to live in and that you have everything they will need to be happy and well looked after. Here are some things to consider:

A suitably sized home

Hamsters are very active animals and they need space and a stimulating environment if they are to live a happy and healthy life. Hamsters need enough room to run, forage, climb and stretch, especially at night when they are most active, so buy as big a cage as possible. Keeping hamsters in a home that is too small can cause health and behaviour problems.

A hamster's home should have a solid plastic floor with a base that is at least 3–5 centimetres deep with a wire top. Wire sides will allow your hamster to climb around the bars of the cage, which is great exercise. To maximize their living space, think about getting a multi-level home for your hamster. As with the base, make sure each floor is solid rather than made from wire bars. You can place tunnels and toys in the home for your hamster to explore.

When choosing a home for your hamster, make sure that it is safe from hazards, such as sharp metal or gaps they could get stuck in. You will also need to make sure that it is secure, as hamsters can easily escape from poorly ▶

constructed cages. Remember to always get the right cage for your hamster's type; for example, a cage that is suitable for a Syrian hamster may not be suitable for a dwarf type, as they could squeeze through the bars. You should also inspect the housing regularly and replace any parts that are damaged or dangerous. For more information on suitable homes for hamsters, see www.rspca.org.uk/hamsters/environment.

Peace and quiet

Hamsters need a comfortable, dry, draught-free and clean place to live, in a quiet place where they can rest undisturbed. Hamsters are very sensitive to high-frequency sound (known as 'ultrasound'), which we cannot hear, and can find it stressful. Position your hamster's cage away from household items that can generate ultrasound, such as television sets, computer screens, vacuum cleaners or sources of running water. Hamsters are also sensitive to light, so place your pet's home in a spot out of direct sunlight and try to make sure that lights go off at approximately the same time each night.

A nesting box or shelter

Your hamster will also need a nesting box or shelter in their home to retreat to where they can keep warm, feel safe and sleep. Make sure this is big enough for your hamster to store food placed nearby, and for them to make a nest and move around comfortably. The shelter should be dark inside – some have an entrance via an angled tube, which prevents light entering. It is better if the shelter does not have a floor, but instead just rests on top of the nesting material so that you can check on your hamster by carefully lifting it up. A tinted red shelter will appear very dark to your hamster, but will enable you to see in without disturbing them.

Suitable bedding

Hamsters love burrowing, so you should line their home with a thick layer of bedding material in the base of the

LEFT: Buy as big a cage as possible. When transporting your hamsters, try to keep them in their own cage. RIGHT: Line your hamster's home with a thick layer of bedding.

cage. You can use several different things as litter material, including coarse sand, dust-free non-cedar wood shavings or granulated corn-cob. Do not use straw, as this can injure their cheek pouches. Make sure that you check the material is free from harmful preservatives and other chemicals. For further tips on suitable bedding go to www.rspca.org.uk/hamsters/environment.

Nesting material

Your hamster will need enough suitable nesting material so that they can make a cup-shaped nest to sleep in. You can give your hamster materials such as good-quality hay, wood wool, shredded paper or cardboard. Do not use materials that can separate into thin strands, such as cotton wool or similar 'fluffy' bedding products, because these can get caught around the hamster's toes or feet and injure them.

Cleaning

It is important to keep your hamster's home clean and supplied with dry bedding and nesting materials, but this needs to be balanced with the need to avoid disturbing your hamster too much, which can be very stressful for them.

Your hamster's bedding material should not be allowed to become damp or very smelly, as this can be bad for their health. Because hamsters communicate using smells, whenever you are cleaning out their home, always put some of the old, unsoiled bedding and nesting material to one side. Once cleaning is complete, return the old unsoiled bedding to their home so that it smells familiar, especially if you have a group of hamsters living together. Make sure that any objects that are soiled by faeces or urine are carefully cleaned or replaced.

Toys, exercise and activities

Hamsters need lots of space to exercise, which is why a multi-level cage can be a good choice, as it allows them to climb and explore. Your hamster will also need appropriate objects to play with, such as small boxes and tubes – inner cores from toilet rolls are ideal. A good-quality, solid running wheel can also provide your hamster with exercise opportunities, but make sure it is big enough to prevent your hamster running in an uncomfortable position. Secure the wheel to the side of the cage, with no gaps for your hamster to get their legs or feet trapped. If you have a long- ▶

haired hamster, take extra care to ensure that their hair does not get caught and tangled in the wheel. For more about toys and enrichments, see page 30.

Transporting your hamster

It is very important to think about how you will transport your hamster safely when you are bringing them home or taking them to the vet. Travelling can be very stressful for hamsters, so it should be avoided unless absolutely necessary. There are several ways in which you can make their journey more comfortable and ensure that they are safe in your vehicle.

You must make sure that you provide for all your hamster's welfare needs as well as minimizing the stress of transportation. Ideally, your hamster should travel in their cage if possible. If you need to transfer them to a smaller cage for the journey, provide familiar-smelling bedding material for comfort and place used, unsoiled nesting material in the carrier with a shelter. This will reassure your hamster while they are on the move. Avoid placing anything in the cage that could injure your pet. A cardboard carrier is not a good idea, because your hamster could chew through it and easily escape, or it could disintegrate if it gets wet.

Hamsters that live in a group should be transported together. If you transfer them to a smaller cage, make sure it is large enough for them all. Travelling together eases the journey and also means that any unfamiliar scents in the carrier will be transferred to all of your hamsters, which can avoid any problems and the need for pets to be reintroduced after a time apart. Cover the cage if you can, so that it is dark for them, but make sure that it still allows enough air in and out.

Make sure your hamster has access to food and water – food can be given as nuggets. To avoid spills and the cage flooding, provide water in the form of small pieces of fruit or vegetables, unless it is a long journey.

It can get unbearably hot in a car on a sunny day, even when it is not that warm, so be aware of this when you are transporting your hamster. Do not leave them alone in a vehicle, as the temperature can quickly soar to unbearable levels, which can be fatal. Ensure the vehicle is kept cool and well ventilated and avoid travelling during the hottest part of the day.

When your hamster is back home, if you have transported them in a smaller cage return them to their home and give them time to rest without being disturbed. This is particularly important when they come home for the first time, so they can get used to their new surroundings. You can download an advice sheet on transporting hamsters from www.rspca.org.uk/hamsters/health.

Holiday time

To avoid unnecessary and stressful journeys for your hamsters when you go away on holiday, it is much better for your pet if you can find a responsible adult who can care for and meet all their welfare needs in your own home.

Introduce them before you go so that you know the responsible adult can safely handle your hamster and has all the information needed to care for your pet. Keep your hamster in their own cage and leave the usual food for the carer to feed them. Make sure that whoever is caring for your pet knows how to check your hamster every day for signs of illness or injury – in a group of hamsters one may suffer an injury as a result of fighting. You should also ensure that the carer knows how to clean out the cage and how regularly this needs to be done.

Tunnels, toys and wheels will enrich your hamster's environment.

Diet

2

Scatter food to encourage foraging behaviour.

What to feed your hamster

A healthy diet

To stay fit and healthy your hamster needs constant access to fresh, clean water and a well-balanced diet. In the wild, hamsters eat a mixture of seeds, cereals, insect larvae and larger insects such as crickets. Pet hamsters need a good-quality, balanced diet that contains all the essential nutrients and minerals; in general, it is best to choose a commercial food suitable for hamsters, which will meet these needs.

How much each hamster needs to eat depends on their age, lifestyle and general health. If you have any concerns or queries about feeding, your vet can give you detailed advice on what, and how much, to feed your hamster.

Feeding time

In the wild, hamsters may range as far as 5 miles while foraging for food, which they carry back to their home in their cheek pouches. Try to encourage natural ▶

food-gathering behaviour by scattering the food around their home. Your hamster will forage for food and carry it to their food store (larder), which is often in the nest box. This will help keep your hamster busy and active, too. If you choose to use a dish for your pet's food, buy one that is flat and make sure it is kept clean by washing it regularly. If your hamster tips up the food dish, try scatter-feeding instead.

If your hamster toilets in one corner of their cage, avoid scattering food in that area. Fresh food that is soiled or brown should be removed from your hamster's home and also from their food store to stop it spoiling.

Whether you scatter-feed or use a dish, it is very important to follow the guidelines on the packet to ensure you do not overfeed your hamster. Overfeeding can lead to weight gain and health issues.

Water bottles

It is best to give your hamster water in a bottle, as a bowl or dish is likely to be tipped and will make the home wet. Choose a bottle with a valveless sipper tube, as hamsters are not able to suck strongly and may find the traditional ball-valve sipper tube difficult to drink from. As long as the sipper is of a relatively small diameter, or has been manufactured with a pinch in the segment, your hamster will find it far easier to use. This may be particularly important for young, old or sick animals.

Make sure you check your hamster's water bottle daily for leaks or blockages, and change the water at least once a day. You should also make time to regularly clean the bottle and nozzle properly to avoid contamination.

The first few days

Usually, a breeder or rescue centre will provide detailed information that will tell you what type of food your hamster has been eating so far and will outline their feeding routine. Some may supply a few days' food for your hamster. Whenever possible, follow the breeder's feeding notes while your new hamster is settling in, and stick to the type of food and routine they are used to. Any changes in a hamster's diet should only be made gradually, as a sudden swap in brand or type of food can lead to an upset stomach. If you have any concerns or queries about feeding, your vet will be able to give you detailed advice on what, and how much, to feed your pet.

A balanced diet

Your hamster needs a good-quality, balanced diet. You can offer commercial hamster foods, which are specially formulated to give your pet all the necessary nutrients and minerals needed to stay happy and healthy, or you can provide a mixture of different seeds, grains, nuts, washed fruit and vegetables. Apple, carrot, pear and broccoli are ideal. Do not suddenly change your hamster's diet, or allow food to become stale, as this can lead to an upset stomach.

Health watch

Keep an eye on how much your hamster eats and drinks. If they start to eat less food than usual, their droppings become moist or their hindquarters become soiled, take your hamster to the vet straight away.

Wet food

Only give wet or powdered food if a vet advises this; for example, because of a dental problem. If a hamster is sick and requires wet food, it is important that new food is given at least twice a day and all traces are removed to ensure the food does not start to go mouldy.

LEFT: A hamster transporting food. ABOVE: Choose a bottle with a valveless sipper tube.

Treats

In the wild, hamsters occasionally eat insects. An alternative to the protein that they get from this part of their natural diet may be offered once or twice a week in the form of small pieces of hard-boiled egg or low-fat cottage cheese. Treats should be limited to food items that are high in protein but low in fat, so avoid other types of cheese. Do not feed your hamster sugary treats, as some hamsters are prone to diabetes. For variety, you can offer your hamster small quantities of greens, cleaned root vegetables or pieces of fruit such as apples, but remove them from the home and the food store if they are not eaten and become soiled or go brown.

ABOVE: Sunflower seeds are high in fat, so only give them as an occasional treat. TOP: Small amounts of carrot can be a treat as part of a balanced diet.

Adding interest

As well as scattering food around your hamster's cage to encourage foraging, you can hide food in tunnels and small boxes, which will also make mealtimes more interesting for them.

Weight watch

It is a good idea to keep a careful eye on your hamster's weight. You can help your hamster to maintain a healthy weight by limiting treats – especially sweet ones such as apple and carrot – and by ensuring that they are not over-fed. It is important to remember that young hamsters and pregnant and nursing females will have different needs to other hamsters. Ask your vet for advice on how to give your hamster a balanced diet and whether you need to adjust their food to help them to achieve a healthy weight.

New foods

Do not make any sudden dietary changes; instead, offer small pieces of a new treat gradually to avoid stomach upsets. Symptoms of indigestion include bloating and lethargy. Following the offering of a new treat, if food consumption falls, faeces become moist or your hamster's hindquarters become soiled, you should seek immediate veterinary treatment. Your vet can advise you on what is safe, but if you are in any doubt, leave it out!

Eating droppings

Hamsters produce two types of droppings. You might see a hamster eating softer droppings directly from their bottom. Eating these is an essential part of all hamsters' diets, because it helps them to get as much goodness as possible from their food. Your hamster will also produce waste in the form of hard droppings.

Things to avoid

A number of foods, such as grapes and rhubarb, are poisonous to hamsters and could make your pet very ill. Citrus fruits should also be avoided as they are too acidic. If you are not sure whether something is safe for your hamster to eat, do not give it to them, as it may be toxic. You can find out more about poisonous substances on page 43. If you think your hamster may have eaten something poisonous, speak to your vet immediately.

Offer new foods in small amounts.

Behaviour

3

Your hamster needs time out of their cage every day.

Hamster behaviour

Sleep

Hamsters rest and sleep during the day, so it is really important that they are not disturbed during this time, or kept in a room where the lights are left on until late at night. In the wild, hamsters are extremely good diggers and they construct deep, dark underground burrows. So make sure your hamster has a thick layer of bedding in which they can carry out these natural burrowing behaviours.

Staying fit and healthy

Hamsters are extremely active and require lots of room in their home so that they can behave normally: running, climbing, digging and burrowing. Your hamster should have plenty of toys and activities to engage them, as well as a nest or shelter to retreat to when they want to rest, or if they feel threatened.

Your hamster needs regular and frequent opportunities to exercise when they are active, which is during the evening or at night. Make sure your hamster has an interesting environment, in which there is plenty to do. This will give your pet plenty of mental and physical stimulation, which means they are more likely to remain fit, healthy and happy.

Being sociable

Syrian hamsters are, by nature, solitary animals, so they should not be kept in pairs or groups. Other types, such as Winter White Russians, can be kept in groups, but they will need careful monitoring to ensure that there are no squabbles. Make sure that you have taken advice from your vet or a qualified animal behaviourist if you are planning to keep ▶

a group of hamsters. If your hamsters are having problems living together, they will need to be separated quickly to avoid the risk of fighting, which could leave your pets seriously injured.

Hamsters can enjoy interacting with people who handle them carefully and are sympathetic to their needs. Remember that for all hamsters their previous environment and experiences will determine their needs and how sociable they are.

In the wild, hamsters travel long distances at night, and therefore they require considerable exercise in captivity. A cage should never be a hamster's sole and permanent home, and it is important that your pet is allowed to exercise outside their cage on a regular basis. However, this should always be supervised and take place in a safe and secure environment, where your hamster cannot escape or come to harm – for example, by chewing electrical cables.

Let your hamster have time out of their cage once you feel you can handle them with confidence. You should always stay with your hamster when they are out of the cage. Never leave them unattended if you have another pet, such as a cat or a dog, because they are natural predators of small animals and they could frighten, harm or even kill your hamster, either deliberately or accidentally.

Scent-marking

Scent-marking is important for hamsters. They mark their territory using secretions from scent glands on their hips to make their home smell familiar and reassuring. These scents are not detected by people, though. When you are cleaning your hamster's home you must make sure that you transfer some of the old, unsoiled nesting and bedding material back into the cage. This ensures that their home still smells familiar and safe, and it is especially important if you have hamsters housed together. If you have a group of hamsters and one of them needs to see the vet, transport them all together so that scents remain familiar. This helps to avoid potential problems associated with reintroducing hamsters after time apart. For more on transporting your hamster safely, see page 18.

Hibernation

In the wild, hamsters hibernate in the winter, but they do wake up during this time to feed. Usually, pet hamsters do not hibernate, as artificial lighting and heating prevent it. If your hamster starts to hibernate, do not disturb them, unless you believe they are unwell. Make sure that your hamster has plenty of fresh water, fresh food and nesting material, as they may wake up to feed during hibernation. Check them

LEFT: Toys help your hamster to stay active and healthy. BELOW LEFT: A wooden chew block. ABOVE: Check your hamster regularly if they hibernate.

regularly and if you are at all unsure, contact your vet for advice.

When there are problems

Every hamster is different and the way they behave will depend upon their age, as well as their personality and experiences. It is important to make sure that you are very familiar with your hamster's normal behaviour and routine. If you notice any changes, you should speak to your vet for detailed advice, as it could be a sign that your hamster is frightened, bored, ill or in pain.

These signs may include: changes in their eating, drinking or toileting habits; hiding; being aggressive; sitting hunched; being reluctant to move; or chewing the bars of the cage. Chewing bars is a natural behaviour, but if you notice that your hamster is chewing excessively, do not be tempted to paint the bars

of their home with chemical deterrents. Although it may stop this behaviour, it could make your pet frustrated, as it does not tackle the cause of the excessive gnawing. Instead, you should look at what is lacking in your pet's environment or diet and try to enrich it, as well as providing a bigger home.

If you see any changes in the behaviour of your hamster, consult your vet so they can give them a check-up and rule out any illness or injury as the cause. Your vet may refer you to an animal behaviourist for advice. You can find links to information about animal behaviourists on page 47, or by going to www.rspca. org.uk/findabehaviourist.

Never shout at or punish your hamster, as they are very unlikely to understand and may become more nervous or scared. If your hamster's behaviour becomes an ongoing problem, talk to an expert.

Toys

Providing toys not only enriches your hamster's environment, but also allows them to perform normal behaviours such as foraging, digging and burrowing. There are many inexpensive ways of adding various items to their enclosure for them to explore. As you get to know your hamster, you should experiment by adding different toys to the cage until you find out which ones they like best.

Remember that you should not go toy mad. Do not fill your hamster's cage with so many items that they can no longer exercise easily.

Here are some toy ideas to try with your hamster:

A WHEEL A good-quality running wheel can give your hamster extra opportunities to exercise, but this should not be the only toy in your hamster's cage, because they need a variety of things to play with to keep the environment interesting. A wheel that is too small will mean your hamster is running with a bent back. As well as being uncomfortable for your pet, this can also lead to back problems or injury. Make sure, therefore, that you buy the largest running wheel or disc that you can find. It is important that the wheel does not overwhelm the floor of the cage – another reason why your pet's home must be large enough to allow space for them to be active and move around comfortably.

The running wheel must be a solid structure fixed close to the cage wall without an axle. This is important to make sure that your hamster's legs or feet do not get caught and injured. The running surface should be non-slip. You should check your hamster's feet regularly. If they are sore, remove the wheel temporarily and ask your vet for advice.

CARDBOARD Boxes with holes cut into them make great hiding places. Hiding part of your hamster's daily food allowance in a cardboard box can also encourage your pet to forage and explore.

TUNNELS You can purchase hamster tunnels made from plastic or other materials such as seagrass. They can also be made from cardboard boxes and the inner cardboard cores from toilet rolls.

ITEMS TO CHEW Hamsters need to gnaw to help their teeth stay at a healthy length. Make sure your hamster has access to a wooden chew block made from non-toxic, untreated wood such as apple wood. There are plenty of things to choose from, from wooden sticks to toys.

HAMSTER BALLS These are not recommended by the RSPCA. Hamster balls may cause your pet stress and could leave them at risk of an injury. Because hamsters have poor eyesight, they rely on their other senses, such as hearing and smell, when they are moving around. Being enclosed in a plastic ball may be stressful for them because it restricts the use of the senses, and they do not have access to food and water. The exercise ball colliding with objects such as furniture may be frightening, and there is also the potential risk of injury to

your hamster's paws or legs if they get pinched or caught in the air holes of the ball. For more on exercise balls go to www.rspca.org.uk/hamsters/health.

SAFETY FIRST Make sure any items you put in your hamster's home are safe and suitable for your pet. Materials should be non-toxic, with smooth, rounded edges. Inspect toys regularly and discard any that are damaged or dangerous.

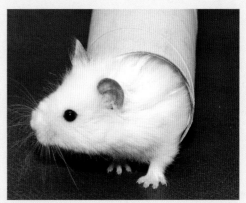

TOP LEFT: Buy the largest wheel you can find. ABOVE: Tunnels also add interest to your hamster's home.

Company

4

Young littermates are the most successful group-housed hamsters.

Being with others

Hamsters are generally solitary and can be aggressive towards other animals, which can result in serious injury or death. This is particularly true of Syrian and Chinese hamsters, and because they are not naturally sociable animals they are better kept on their own.

More than one pet

If you would like to keep more than one hamster, it is not enough to keep them in separate cages next to each other. Both male and female hamsters produce strong odours that they use to communicate. Although they are not detectable to humans, the hamster's keen sense of smell means that they will pick up on the scents of other animals nearby and this can be very stressful for them. It is much better, therefore, to choose a different type of hamster that can live in a group instead.

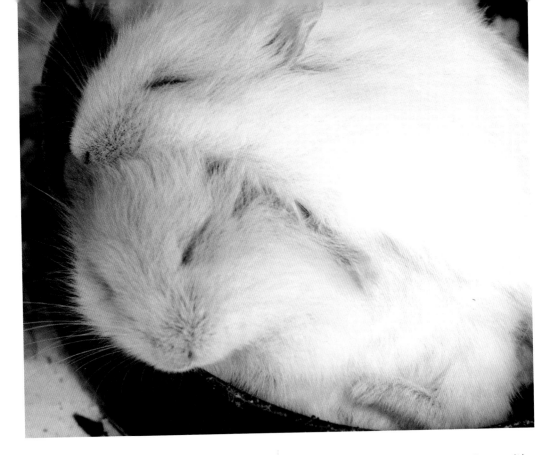

Other pets in the home

A hamster's sensitivity to smell and the fact that it is naturally a prey species means that it is also important not to allow other animals too close to a hamster's cage. You should never allow another pet to sit on your hamster's home or interfere with it. Do not leave your pets alone together unsupervised, even if your hamster is in their cage, as accidents may happen.

Good groups

With the appropriate advice from a vet or rehoming centre, it is possible to keep some hamster types, such as Winter White Russians, in pairs or trios. However, this must be done with care. The groups must be formed early in life and it is important that no new animals are added to the group at a later date.

The most successful group-housed hamsters are young littermates, as this will help to reduce the risk of aggression. It is best if the pair or trio is a single-sex group, to avoid unwanted pregnancies.

A home for a group

If you are giving a home to a pair or trio of littermates, you will need to provide a cage with lots of space and give them plenty of things to play with, such as wheels, toys, clean hay, shredded paper and pieces of tissue. You should also provide plenty of places for all your hamsters to hide. It is vital that you check all your hamsters every morning for signs of injury, because if fighting occurs it is more likely to take place at night, during their most active period. If you are worried about your hamsters fighting or you find one of your hamsters is injured, consult your vet immediately. As well as discussing treatment of any injuries, they will be able to give you advice on how to deal with aggression. For further information on housing hamsters in groups go to www.rspca.org. uk/hamsters/company.

You and your hamster

A good relationship with your hamster can be rewarding for both you and your pet, and will also make it easier when you take your hamster for routine veterinary examinations and carrying out health checks.

Get into a routine of handling your hamster gently every day from an early age. Hamsters can enjoy interacting with people who handle them carefully and are sympathetic to their needs, but they can become frightened and aggressive if they feel threatened.

A hamster may not be used to being handled, or may have been handled roughly in the past, so they may find human contact distressing. With time and patience you can help your hamster to grow more confident and comfortable around people. If you are concerned about anything to do with handling your pet, ask your vet or a qualified animal behaviourist for advice.

Hamsters and children

Many families with children keep hamsters. Having a pet can improve a child's social skills and caring for ▶

LEFT TO RIGHT: With advice it is possible to keep some types of hamster as a group. A trio of littermates. Handle your hamster gently every day.

an animal can encourage kindness, understanding and responsibility. While children will quickly learn to treat a new hamster as part of the family, it is important to teach them to be very gentle as a hamster can be injured easily through rough or careless handling, due to their small size and delicate bones. Always supervise your children when they are handling your hamster and minimize the risk of them accidentally dropping your pet by getting them to sit on the ground to pet or hold them. Only adults and responsible older children should be allowed to pick up your hamster, to reduce the risk of injury if they are mishandled or accidentally dropped.

Safety first

Never leave your hamster unsupervised with another animal or person who may deliberately or accidentally harm or frighten them. When you are away, make sure your hamster is properly cared for by a responsible person who can give your pet the care and company they need.

If your hamster shows any changes in behaviour or regular signs of stress or fear, such as hiding or aggression when they are being handled, you should seek expert advice. It is important to get your hamster checked by a vet first to rule out any form of illness or injury that could be causing their reaction. Your vet can then refer you to a behaviour expert.

Handling your hamster

Hamsters can find being picked up and handled stressful because in the wild they are a prey species. Learning to handle your hamster correctly will ensure that they do not view you as a threat.

A hamster's reaction to handling will depend on their past experiences, so it is important to be patient. This will allow them to grow more confident and comfortable around you. Always move slowly and talk quietly around your hamster, to avoid startling them.

Try to get into a routine with your hamster so that they get used to being handled regularly. Do not try to cram all of your interaction time into one handling period at the weekend – it should be more frequent and part of your hamster's regular daily routine. Make sure you choose a time when your hamster is not resting or sleeping – disturbing hamsters when they are at rest in the day can cause them stress.

Learn to handle your hamster correctly so that your pet does not feel anxious, and allow them to investigate your hands in their own time. Pick up your hamster by cupping them in your

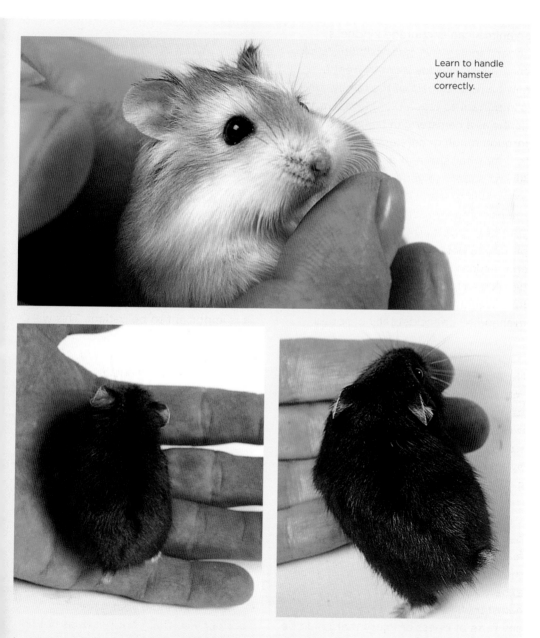

Learn to handle your hamster correctly.

hands and then gently opening your hands so that your hamster is sitting across both palms. For safety, and to avoid falls and injuries, always hold your hamster close to a surface such as a tabletop or your lap.

Health
and welfare

5

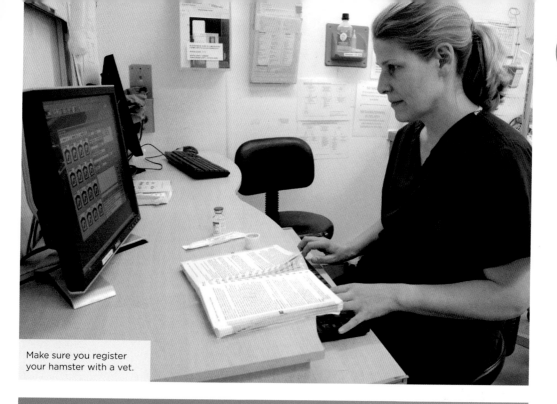

Make sure you register
your hamster with a vet.

Protecting your pet

Hamsters can be vulnerable to a range of
illnesses and their health can deteriorate
very quickly. They are not very good
at showing outward signs of pain or
distress and they may be suffering a
great deal before you notice anything
is wrong. Hamsters can be affected
by many diseases, including infections
from contaminated food, water or
bedding material. Stressed hamsters are
particularly prone to getting ill.

It is important to check every day
that your hamster is behaving normally,
moving around, breathing well and that
they have bright eyes and a shiny coat.
Make sure that someone else does this if

you are away. If you or someone caring
for your hamster suspect that they
are in pain, ill or injured, contact your
vet immediately.

Find a vet and arrange insurance
It is important that you find a vet with
whom you can register your new hamster,
and book them in for a check-up. The vet
will be able to give you lots of information
on looking after your hamster. You can
read more about finding a vet and low-
cost vet care at www.rspca.org.uk/
whatwedo/vetcare.

Check the insurance situation, too.
Some charities and breeders may provide ▶

◀ a short period of insurance cover, which you can either take over and extend, or you may want to arrange an alternative policy. Where insurance is not provided, it is a good idea to consider arranging for a policy to start from the moment you bring home the hamster. This will cover you for unexpected vets' bills in the future and can safeguard your pet's health.

Health checks

Take your hamster for a routine health check with your vet at least once a year. It is a good chance to ask for advice about things you can do to protect your hamster's health. The vet can also check your hamster for signs of dental disease and have a look at their nails. However, don't forget that you should be checking their nails and teeth regularly at home.

Changes in behaviour

A boring environment, stress, frustration or lack of mental stimulation can lead to hamsters developing repetitive behaviours such as running in circles or gnawing the cage bars for long periods of time.

If you notice behaviours like these, try getting a bigger cage for your hamster and providing them with more toys and activities. It is also important to check that your hamster is not being disturbed by the rest of the household, especially children and other pets, and that they are not being woken up when they are sleeping. If your hamster continues to show repetitive behaviours, seek the advice of your vet, who may refer you to a qualified animal behaviourist.

Hibernation

Your hamster may begin to hibernate in winter. If this happens, make sure there is always fresh food and water available for when they wake up. For more on hibernation, see page 28.

Grooming

If your hamster is long-haired, make sure their coat is kept clean and un-matted by regular combing and brushing. Ask a pet-care specialist for advice if you are unsure how to groom your hamster properly.

Teeth and nails

Hamsters' teeth grow continually throughout their lives, so they need to gnaw objects to keep their teeth sharp and regularly worn down. If one incisor tooth is damaged, the other can keep growing and may eventually stop your hamster eating. Check your hamster's claws and teeth regularly, at least once a week. If teeth or nails become overgrown or damaged, contact your vet for advice. ▶

Daily checks

Check your hamster carefully every day.

it might mean that they have gone off their food so they may need a check-up with your vet. If you suspect your hamster is in pain, ill or injured, or you notice any of the following signs, you should contact your vet immediately.

- Not eating or drinking
- Sitting in a hunched-up position
- Sunken or dull-looking eyes
- Disinterested at times when normally active
- Drinking lots of water
- Wet faeces and/or diarrhoea (which may lead to soiling of their bottom)
- Discharge from the nostrils, eyes or vagina
- Persistent sneezing or coughing
- Persistent scratching, especially if focused on one area
- Suddenly more aggressive than usual
- Firm, warm and swollen stomach
- Any injuries or abnormal lumps
- Difficulty walking or unsteady balance
- Not using a limb

Check your hamster every day to make sure they are fit and healthy. Make sure your pet is behaving normally, moving around easily, breathing well and has bright eyes and a shiny coat. When you are handling your hamster, run your fingers gently over their body to check for lumps and bumps. It is also a good opportunity to check that they have not lost or gained weight. If you can feel your hamster's bones more than usual,

◀ Fur loss

If you notice your hamster has areas of fur loss, there could be a number of causes for this. A hamster that scratches or rubs its coat on the bars of its cage excessively may have mites. They cause extreme irritation and distress to animals, so prompt veterinary treatment is essential. If your hamster displays symptoms that suggest they may have a mite problem, take them to the vet immediately for treatment. Fur loss can also be caused by other issues such as lack of protein, stress, disease, or, if they are housed in a group, fighting. Whatever the cause, it is important to speak to your vet for advice and treatment if necessary.

Wet tail

Diarrhoea is considered one of the most common digestive problems in hamsters. It is most likely to be seen in hamsters that are stressed, due to being transported or living in an overcrowded cage, for example. Hamsters can suffer from a condition called 'wet tail'. It can be highly infectious, so if your hamsters are housed in a group, it could spread rapidly, causing watery diarrhoea which leaves a hamster's fur around the tail, belly and behind wet and matted – hence the name 'wet tail'. If you notice these signs you should ask your vet for advice immediately.

Constipation

There are several reasons why your hamster may become constipated, for example because they have tapeworms, or if they eat their bedding and it causes a blockage. If you notice your hamster's eating habits have changed, the quantity of their droppings reduces or stops, or if they have loose droppings, ask your vet for advice immediately – your pet could be seriously ill.

Colds

Hamsters are highly vulnerable to strains of the human common cold. Do not handle your hamster if you have a cold. If you notice your hamster is sneezing, lethargic or coughing, has loud or laboured breathing, or a runny nose or eyes, see your vet immediately. A cold in a hamster can develop into pneumonia.

Wounds and abscesses

If a hamster has been fighting, or gets injured, a wound can turn into an abscess, which can be very painful. Check your hamster every day for signs of injury or wounds, and if you notice your hamster is injured, contact your vet for advice – tackling wounds as soon as possible minimizes the risk of abscesses forming.

Impaction of the pouches

Impaction happens when your hamster tries to store something unsuitable in its pouches, or tries to store too much and it gets stuck. If you are worried your hamster may have impacted cheek pouches, talk to your vet as they will need to remove whatever is causing it. Make sure you try to reduce the risk of impaction by keeping unsuitable items out of your hamster's cage. For more on suitable items for bedding and litter, see page 16, and for food see page 23.

Falls

Hamsters are by nature climbers and are also quite delicate, so it is possible that they may fall and injure themselves. Make sure you reduce the risk of falls by always handling your hamster carefully. Handling should be done close to a surface like a tabletop or on your lap, to reduce the height they could fall from. Keep a close eye on your hamster and remember to check them every day for signs of injury, such as difficulty walking, unsteady balance or not using a limb. If you suspect that your hamster is in pain, ill or injured, go and see your vet immediately. For more on handling your hamster safely, see pages 36–7.

Poisoning

Preventing your hamster from coming into contact with poisonous substances and treating any accidental poisonings quickly and appropriately is an important part of responsible pet ownership. Common items that are poisonous to hamsters include rodent poisons – also known as 'rodenticides' – ivy, rhubarb and rhubarb leaves, foxgloves, oleander and chocolate.

If you suspect your pet has been poisoned, act fast and contact your nearest vet for advice immediately. For more detailed advice on preventing and dealing with poisoning go to www.rspca.org.uk/poisoning.

CLOCKWISE FROM TOP LEFT: Keep an eye on your hamster's pouches as they can get impacted. Chocolate, foxgloves and rhubarb - all poisonous to hamsters.

Your questions answered

Dr Jane Tyson BSc (Hons) MSc PhD, hamster behaviour and welfare expert, Companion Animals Department, RSPCA

Q: My Syrian hamster has two small lumps on his hips. Should I be worried?
A: The lumps that you can feel on your hamster's hips are probably his scent glands. These produce odours used for communication. These scent glands are found on the hips of Syrian hamsters and on the stomach of dwarf species. They are also more prominent in males than females. Scent glands are sometimes mistaken for tumours, but they are completely normal. However, if you are at all concerned, or they change size, bleed, or produce an unusual discharge, you should talk to your vet.

Q: When I try to hold my hamster he bites me. What can I do differently?
A: Hamsters are timid animals and although they can get used to careful handling, they can become frightened and aggressive when they feel threatened. It is best to ask your vet for advice in case there are any underlying health conditions causing pain or discomfort when your hamster is handled. Try to reduce the stress associated with handling by ensuring you have positive interactions with your pet. By taking your time, you can help your hamster get used to you and become comfortable with gentle handling. Hamsters should not be handled when they are resting or sleeping unless absolutely necessary as they can find this stressful. For more information on handling, see page 36.

Q: My hamster is gnawing at his cage all the time. What is wrong?
A: It is possible that your hamster is bored and needs a more stimulating environment. Have a look

at some of the suggestions on page 30 for toys and other enrichments that you could add to his cage and think about getting a bigger cage if you can. You should also make sure that your hamster has access to a wooden gnawing block or toy to help to keep his teeth at the correct length. Check his front teeth for signs that they are overgrown or damaged and if necessary seek advice from your vet.

Q: I have a pair of Winter White Russian hamsters that I have had for a year or so. Is it okay to add a new hamster to the group?
A: No, it is not advisable. Hamsters are very territorial and even types that live in groups in the wild, such as Winter White Russians, will not accept a new hamster into an established pair or group. It is extremely likely that they would fight and could severely injure each other, so it is best avoided. For more on groups, see page 34.

Q: How can I make sure my hamster's life is as stress-free as possible?
A: Hamsters that are stressed are much more likely to become ill, so it is very sensible to try to minimize unnecessary stress. You can do this by making sure your hamster's home is placed in a quiet, draught-free part of the home where disturbances will be kept to a minimum while they are sleeping. You should also ensure that you do not transport your hamster unless it is absolutely necessary. Keep a close eye on your hamster's behaviour, eating and drinking habits and droppings. If any of these change or they are showing signs of fear, stress, boredom or frustration, seek advice from your vet or a qualified animal behaviourist.

LEFT: Excessive gnawing can be due to boredom or stress. ABOVE: Minimize stress to help keep your hamster happy and healthy.

Index

Resources

RSPCA

For more information and advice from the RSPCA about caring for your hamster, go to www.rspca.org.uk/hamsters.

Veterinary advice

- Find a vet: Advice on finding low-cost veterinary care at www.rspca.org.uk/findavet.
- Vet Help Direct at www.vethelpdirect.com.
- Vetfone (24-hour service) at www.vetfone.co.uk.
- Find a Vet at www.findavet.rcvs.org.uk/home.

Behaviour Advice

- Advice on finding a behaviourist at www.rspca.org.uk/findabehaviourist.
- The Association for the Study of Animal Behaviour (ASAB) at www.asab.org.
- The Association of Pet Behaviour Counsellors (APBC) at www.apbc.org.uk.
- If you are concerned about your hamster's behaviour, contact a major rescue organization or rehoming centre, such as the RSPCA, for expert advice. They will be happy to help you, even if you have not adopted your pet from their rehoming centre.

PET GUIDE

Learn more about other popular pets with these bestselling RSPCA pet guides

Care for Your Guinea Pigs

Find out what your guinea pigs need to stay happy and healthy

Care for Your Puppy

Find out what your puppy needs to stay happy and healthy

Care for Your Rabbits

Find out what your rabbits need to stay happy and healthy

Care for Your Kitten

Find out what your kitten needs to stay happy and healthy